Published by Creative Paperbacks
P.O. Box 227, Mankato, Minnesota 56002
Creative Paperbacks is an imprint of
The Creative Company
www.thecreativecompany.us

Design by The Design Lab
Production by Chelsey Luther
Art direction by Rita Marshall
Printed in the United States of America

Photographs by Alamy (Jeff Rotman, Travelpix),
Dreamstime (Jmjm, Jinfeng Zhang), Shutterstock (Alex
Fleming, glenda, Eric Isselee, stockshotportfolio),
SuperStock (age fotostock, Minden Pictures, NHPA,
Roberta Olenick/All Canada Photos)

Library of Congress Cataloging-in-Publication Data
Riggs, Kate.
Sea lions / Kate Riggs.
p. cm. — (Amazing animals)
Summary: A basic exploration of the appearance,
behavior, and habitat of sea lions, oceanic mammals
related to seals. Also included is a story from folklore
explaining why Japanese fishers respected sea lions.
Includes bibliographical references and index.
ISBN 978-1-60818-349-4 (hardcover)
ISBN 978-0-89812-928-1 (pbk)
1. Sea lions—Juvenile literature. I. Title. II. Series:
Amazing animals.

QL737.P63R54 2014
599.79'75—dc23   2013002866

First Edition
9 8 7 6 5 4 3 2 1

AMAZING ANIMALS

SEA LIONS

BY KATE RIGGS

CREATIVE
PAPERBACKS

A sea lion is a **mammal** that has flippers for feet. There are six kinds of sea lions. They swim in the **oceans**. Most sea lions are named for the places they live.

mammal an animal that has hair or fur and feeds its babies with milk

oceans big areas of deep, salty water

Sea lions have long bodies that are good for swimming. They have thick skin and fur. Some sea lions look like earless seals. Earless seals have small holes in their head for ears. But sea lions have ear flaps.

Most sea lions live in warm waters, such as near Australia

The biggest sea lions can be 11 feet (3.4 m) long. They weigh 2,000 to 2,500 pounds (907–1,134 kg). The smallest sea lions weigh about 1,000 pounds (454 kg).

Alaska's Steller sea lions
are the largest sea lions

Sea lions rest on sandy beaches sometimes

Sea lions are ocean animals. They live mostly in the water near three **continents**. But they go on land to warm up in the sunshine.

continents Earth's seven big pieces of land

*Fish make up a big
part of a sea lion's diet*

Sea lions eat meat. They eat fish, squid, sea birds, and other ocean animals. Sea lions hunt in the water. They are fast swimmers. They use their sharp teeth to grab **prey**.

prey animals that are killed and eaten by other animals

A mother sea lion gives birth to one **pup**. Mothers and their pups live together on a beach. A sea lion pup has dark brown or black fur. It drinks milk from its mother. Pups learn how to catch fish when they are two months old.

pup a baby sea lion

Sea lions on land live in groups called colonies. Sea lions talk to each other using clicking, chirping, groaning, and barking sounds. A sea lion can live for 20 to 30 years.

Sea lions tell each other where food is and warn of danger

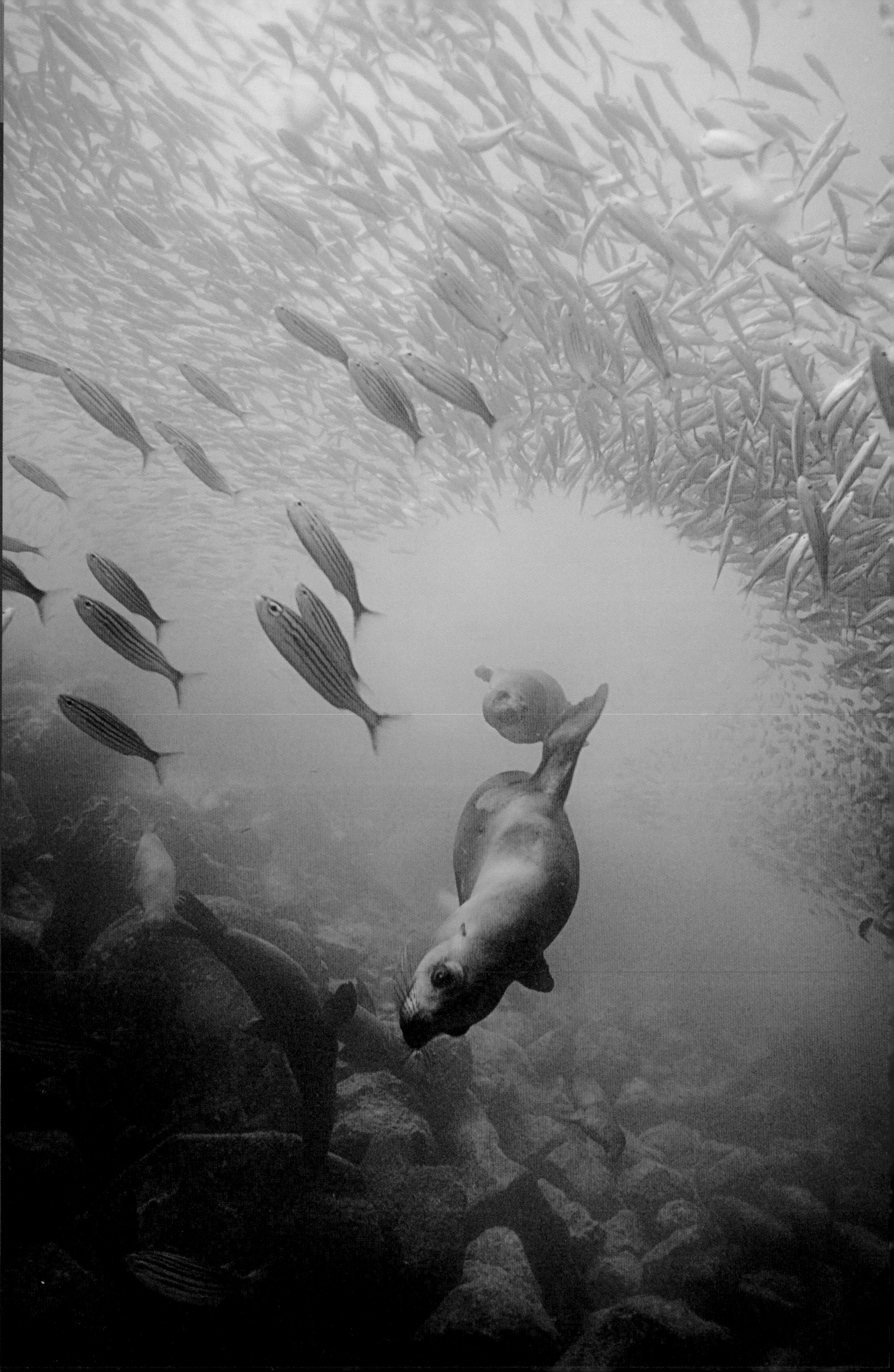

Sea lions swim and hunt together. Sometimes they even sleep in the water! They float on their backs to sleep.

*Pups play and practice
hunting underwater*

People like to watch sea lions in California. Some people go to South America or Australia to see them, too. Other sea lions live in zoos. Many zoo sea lions learn to do tricks. It is fun to watch a sea lion hold a ball on its nose!

Sea lions are smart animals that like to have fun

A *Sea Lion Story*

Why do fishers respect sea lions? People in Japan told a story about this. A fisher once found a pile of fur coats on the shore. He took one coat home. When he went back to the shore, a young woman was there. He married her, and they lived happily. Then one day, the man gave his wife the fur coat. She put it on and became a sea lion! She returned to the sea. And the fisher gave her fish whenever he saw her.

Read More

Hodge, Judith. *Seals, Sea Lions, and Walruses.* Hauppauge, N.Y.: Barron's, 1999.

Sexton, Colleen. *Sea Lions.* Minneapolis, Bellwether Media, 2008.

Websites

National Geographic Kids Coloring Book
http://kids.nationalgeographic.com/kids/activities/moreactivities/coloring-book-animals-a-to-i/
This site has a picture of California sea lions to print out and color.

PBS Kids Dragonfly TV: Sea Lions
http://pbskids.org/dragonflytv/show/sealions.html
Watch this video to find out more about what sea lions eat.

Index